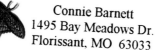

Connie Barnett
1495 Bay Meadows Dr.
Florissant, MO 63033

MW00634225

Quilt Note

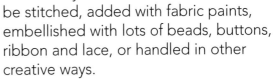

Sunbonnet Sue and Sam have been favorite appliqué and embroidery motifs for stitchers and quilters for many years. These two have been together longer than most married couples.

The patterns in this book show this duo involved in everyday activities, including fun things like skating, building a sand castle, swinging, and even quilting.

You may select any 12 of the 26 patterns given to be stitched in a sampler like the one shown in this book, or choose a combination of patterns to create projects all your own. The patterns given may be stitched in fabric using appliqué techniques or embroidered as outlines. The blocks in the sample quilt were appliquéd with embroidered details. These details may be stitched, added with fabric paints, embellished with lots of beads, buttons, ribbon and lace, or handled in other creative ways.

No matter what method you choose to stitch your quilt, get ready to go back in time to your childhood as you play along with Sue and Sam.

Fun With Sue & Sam

PROJECT SPECIFICATIONS
Skill Level: Intermediate
Quilt Size: 56" x 70"
Block Size: 12" x 12"
Number of Blocks: 12

FABRIC & BATTING
- Assorted scraps for appliqué
- 1¼ yards green print
- 1⅜ yards dark green tonal
- 1½ yards muslin
- Backing 62" x 76"
- Batting 62" x 76"

SUPPLIES & TOOLS
- All-purpose thread in cream and colors to match fabrics
- Quilting thread
- Embroidery floss in assorted colors
- Assorted embellishments such as ribbon, lace, buttons or beads (optional)
- Water-erasable marker or light lead pencil
- Basic sewing and embroidery tools and supplies

Cutting
1. Cut (12) 12½" x 12½" A squares muslin; fold and crease each square to mark the horizontal and vertical centers.

2. Cut three 2½" by fabric width strips dark green tonal; subcut strips into eight 12½" B strips.

3. Cut three 2½" x 40½" C strips dark green tonal.

4. Cut five 2½" by fabric width strips dark green tonal. Join strips on short ends to make one long strip; press seams open. Subcut strip into two 54½" D strips and two 44½" E strips.

5. Cut six 6½" by fabric width strips green print. Join strips on short ends to make one long strip; press seams open. Subcut strips into two 58½" F strips and two 56½" G strips.

6. Cut seven 2¼" by fabric width strips dark green tonal for binding.

7. Prepare templates for appliqué shapes using full-size patterns given; trace shapes onto the wrong side of fabric scraps in selected colors. *Note: Refer to the photo of the quilt for color suggestions for each piece.*

8. Cut out shapes, leaving a ⅛" to ¼" seam allowance all around each piece.

Completing Individual Blocks

1. Using a light box or other light source, transfer appliqué designs to the A squares using creased lines as guides for centering designs.

2. Turn under seam allowance of cut appliqué pieces except where the edge of a piece is overlapped by another piece as shown in Figure 1; baste to hold.

Figure 1

3. Arrange pieces on the marked A squares using traced lines as guides for placement, overlapping pieces as necessary; pin or baste to hold pieces in place.

4. Hand-stitch pieces in place with matching all-purpose thread.

5. Add detailed embroidery stitches to each block, referring to suggestions given in Block Embroidery Suggestions.

Block Embroidery Suggestions

Note: Select floss colors to match realistic images such as blue/gray for ice on pond, green for grass, yellow and black for bumblebee and brown for wooden items or tree trunks.

1. Embroidery patterns given have detail lines that may or may not be added to your blocks. The sample quilt shown has many of the embroidered details, but some were not added. Make the designs your own by adding details to your blocks as desired.

2. When embroidering hatbands, start at the front (face side) of the hat and work toward the back. This allows you to use the long, leftover ends of floss to tie bows or leave ribbon tails.

3. All grass is embroidered using 3 strands of floss and a stem stitch.

4. Sue's hatband is embroidered using a laced running stitch with 6 strands of two colors of floss unless otherwise stated. One color is used for the running stitch and the other is used for the lacing over and under the running stitches. Use both colors to tie a bow at the back of her hat.

5. Sam's hatband is embroidered in either a chain or stem stitch using 6 strands of floss. The buttons are made using French knots, and the tails are formed with a straight stitch. Bows are formed using a lazy-daisy stitch.

6. Ice Skating Together: Embroider outside edge of pond with a stem stitch and 3 strands of floss. Use 2 strands of the same floss to stem-stitch the lines on the ice. Use 2 strands of floss to stem-stitch the mountains and scarf fringe. Use a straight stitch with 2 strands of floss for treetops. Chain-stitch the tree trunks with 2 strands of floss. Outline-stitch the boughs of the trees with 2 strands of floss.

8. Time to Swing: Use 2 strands of floss for the hyacinth stems. Make hyacinth flowers with French knots using 2 strands of floss. Use a lazy-daisy stitch and 2 strands of floss to make the tulip leaves and a stem stitch for the tulip stems. Form the tulip with three lazy-daisy stitches starting at the tips of the flowers, placing the rounded portion at the bottom of the tulip. The rope for the swing was made by couching plastic canvas yarn in place with floss. Use 3 strands of floss to stem-stitch the puddles.

7. Sharing a Heart: A piece of ½"-wide white eyelet lace was stitched under the edges of the heart instead of embroidered loops as shown on the pattern. Tack a piece of ⅛"-wide ribbon to create Sue's hatband; stitch a ribbon rose to the back end. Chain-stitch Sam's hatband using 3 strands of floss and add a French knot and two straight stitches to finish the hat. Use 6 strands of floss and a stem-stitch to make the loop on the heart and create the rug design.

9. Sharing an Umbrella: Use 3 strands of floss and a satin stitch to add details to and frame the umbrella, adding French knots at the bottom tips. The handle was made with one line of chain stitches between two lines of stem stitches using

3 strands of floss. Add a lazy-daisy stitch at the top tip. Use 2 strands of floss and a lazy-daisy stitch for raindrops. **Note:** *In the sample, 1 strand of silver-metallic floss and 1 strand of gray floss were used for the raindrops.*

12. Friends Forever: Stitch hats and grass as instructed on page 2 in steps 1–4.

10. Planting a Tree: Use 1 strand of floss to make stem stitches and French knots to form spout on the watering can. Use 3 strands of floss and a stem stitch to form the handle. Stem-stitch tree with 2 strands of floss and the buds with 1 strand each of two different colors of floss. Stem-stitch hills with 3 strands and the dirt with 2 strands of floss.

13. Building Sand Castles: Stem-stitch sand with 2 strands of floss. Sea shells, shovel and bucket details were stem-stitched with 2 strands of floss. Add two rows of chain stitches in the middle of the bucket handle.

11. Let's Play Ball: Outline-stitch dog with 3 strands of floss. Chain-stitch dog's collar with 2 strands of floss. Outline baseball with stem stitch and 2 strands of floss. Stem-stitch baseball sewn lines with 2 strands of floss.

14. Roasting Marshmallows: Metallic thread was used to create the straight stitches for the stars. Outline marshmallows with 1 strand of floss and satin-stitch the insides with 2 strands of floss. Stem-stitch sticks and smoke with 2 strands and hill with 3 strands of floss. Use 1 strand of three different fire-color flosses to chain-stitch the fire. Chain-stitch the wood with 1 strand each of three different colors.

15. Off to the Garden: Stem-stitch flower stems and flowers with 2 strands of floss. Add wheel spokes using 2 strands of floss and a stem stitch.

16. Be My Honey: Stem-stitch bee and lines on hive using 2 strands of floss. Use 3 strands of floss to stem-stitch handles on buckets. Chain-stitch the bee's body with 2 strands of floss. Stem-stitch wings, legs and antennae using 1 strand of floss.

17. Quilting Friends: Embroider seams of the quilt using a variety of decorative stitches such as herringbone, feather and chevron stitches. Use 3 strands of floss to straight-stitch lines on chairs.

Completing the Top

1. Select and join three appliquéd blocks with two B strips to make a row; press seams toward B. Repeat for four rows.

2. Join the rows with three C strips to complete the quilt center; press seams toward C.

3. Sew a D strip to opposite long sides and E strips to the top and bottom of the quilt center; press seams toward D and E strips.

4. Sew an F strip to opposite sides and G strips to the top and bottom of the quilt center; press seams toward F and G to complete the top.

Finishing the Quilt

1. Mark a 2" diagonal grid on the background of each appliquéd block using the water-erasable marker or light lead pencil.

2. Sandwich the batting between the completed top and prepared backing piece; pin or baste to hold layers together.

3. Quilt on marked lines and as desired by hand or machine.

4. When quilting is complete, remove marked lines, trim edges even and remove pins or basting.

5. Join the binding strips on short ends to make one long strip; press seams open. Fold the strip with wrong sides together; press.

6. Pin the raw edges of the binding strip to the raw edges of the quilt; stitch all around, mitering corners and overlapping ends.

7. Turn the binding to the back side of the quilt; hand- or machine-stitch in place to finish. ∎

Fun With Sue & Sam
Placement Diagram
56" x 70"

HOUSE OF WHITE BIRCHES, BERNE, INDIANA 46711   WWW.WHITEBIRCHES.COM

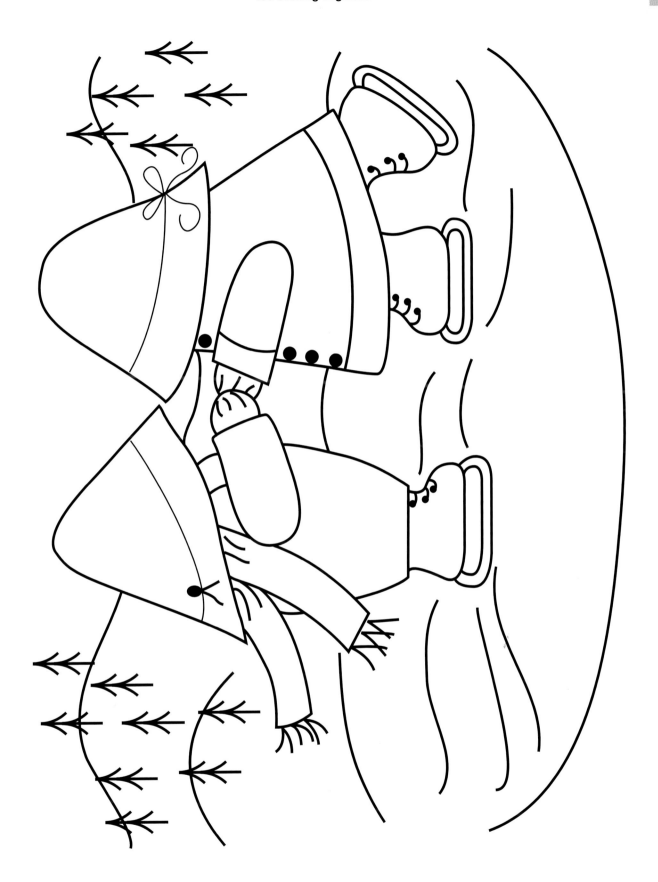

Fun With Sue & Sam   **7**

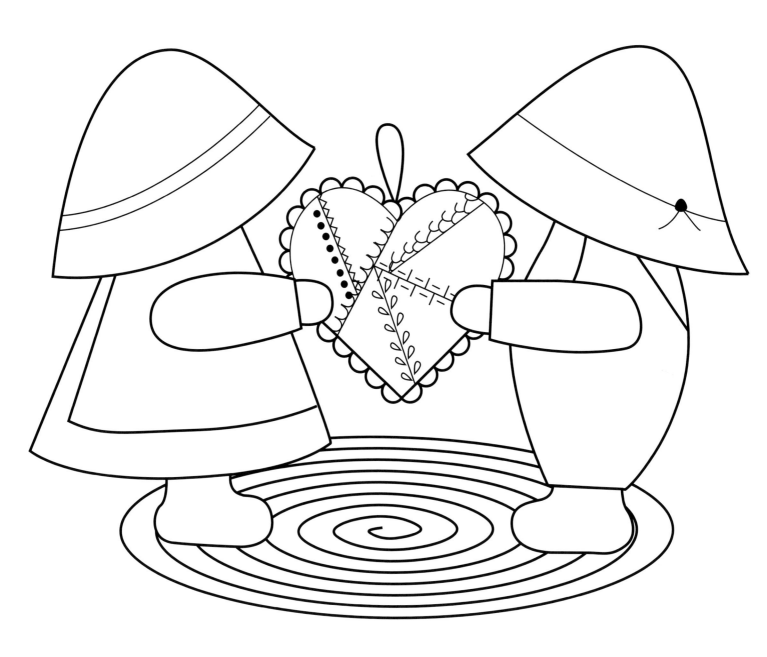

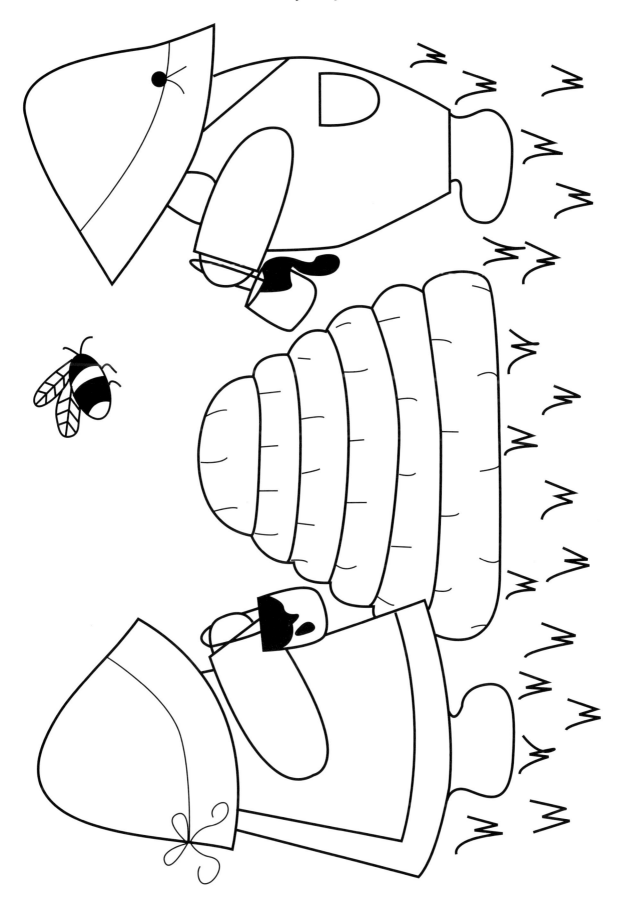

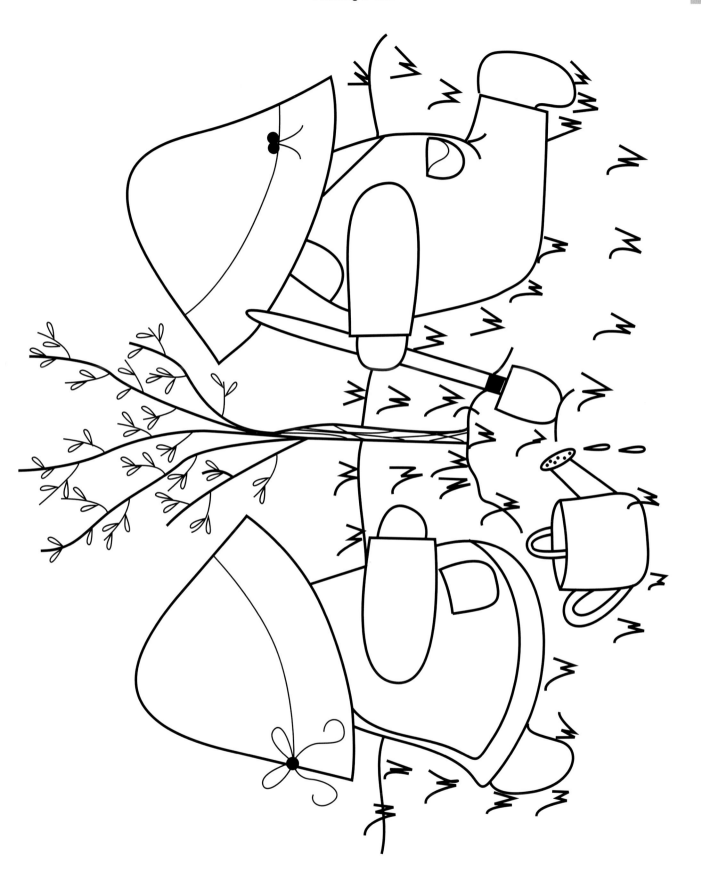

HOUSE OF WHITE BIRCHES, BERNE, INDIANA 46711   WWW.WHITEBIRCHES.COM

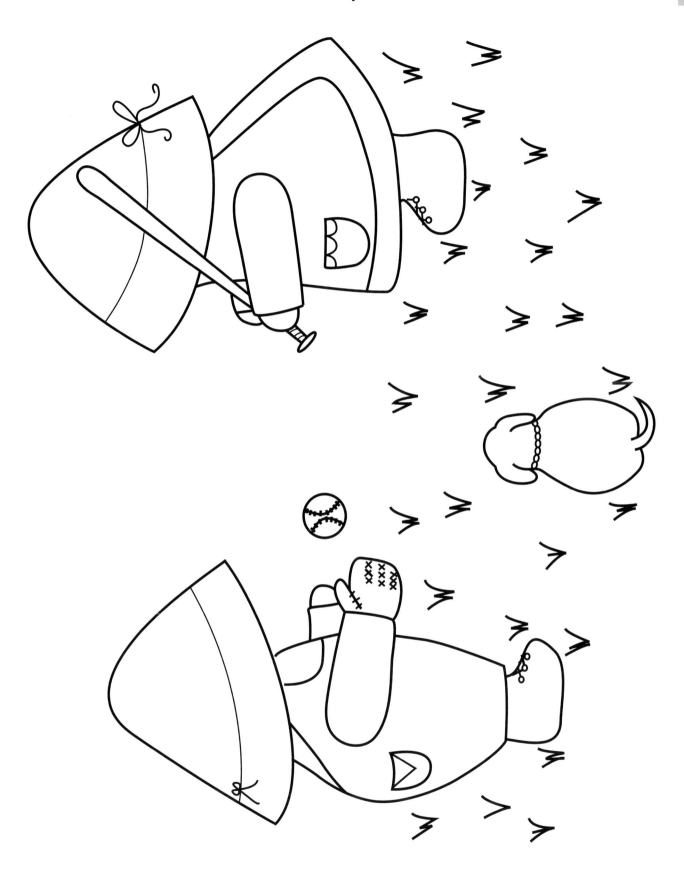

HOUSE OF WHITE BIRCHES, BERNE, INDIANA 46711   WWW.WHITEBIRCHES.COM

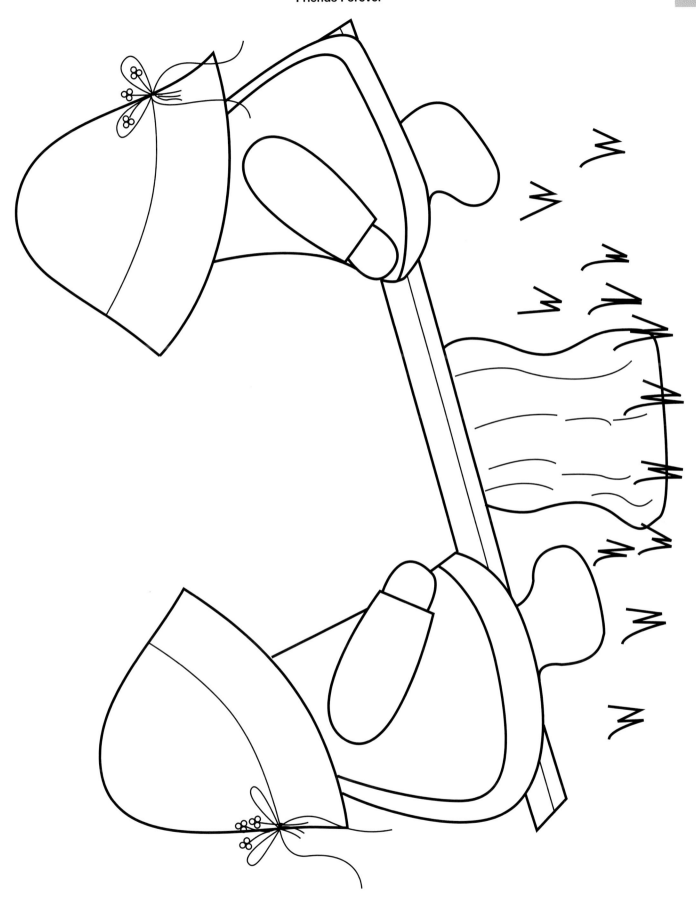

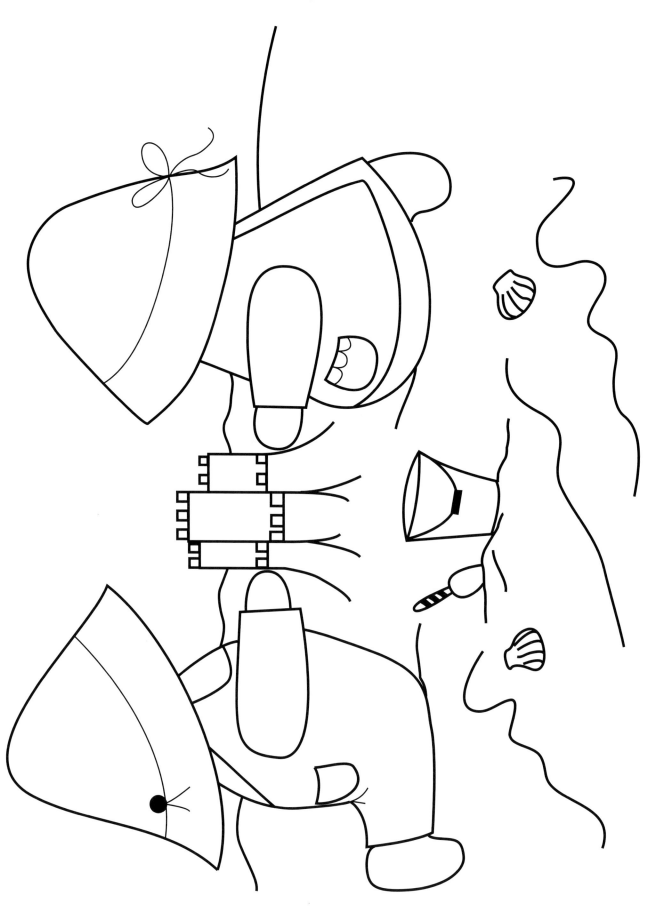

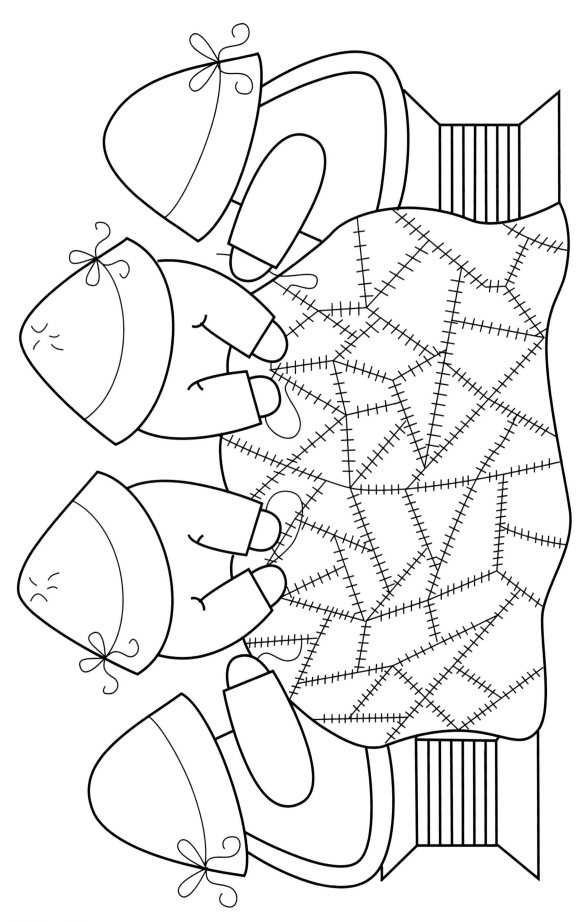

HOUSE OF WHITE BIRCHES, BERNE, INDIANA 46711   WWW.WHITEBIRCHES.COM

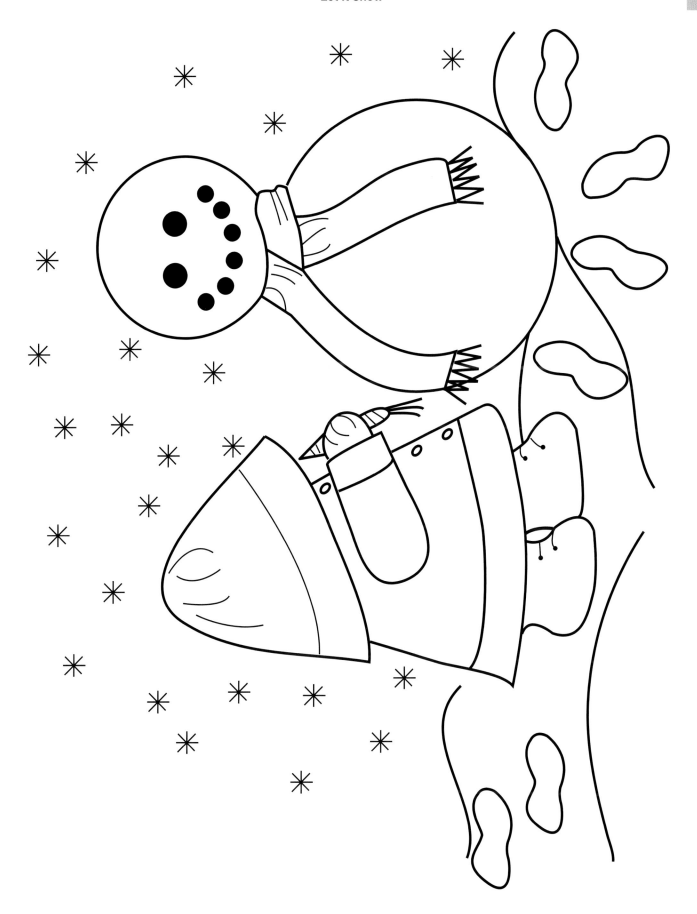

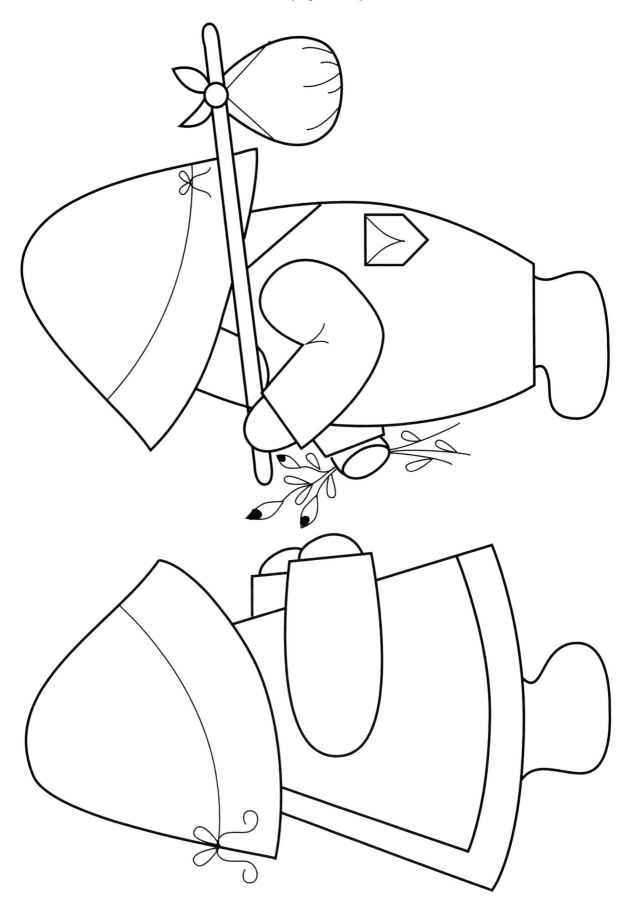

HOUSE OF WHITE BIRCHES, BERNE, INDIANA 46711 WWW.WHITEBIRCHES.COM

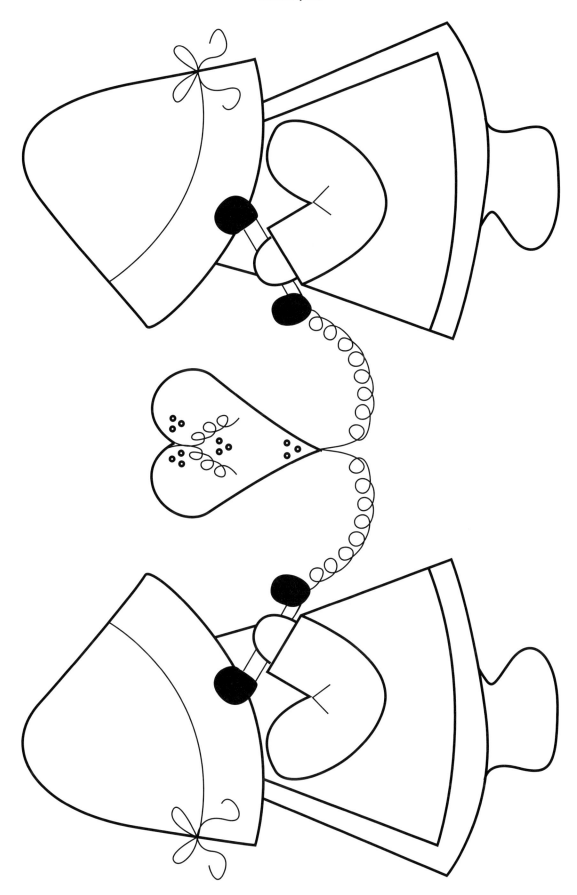

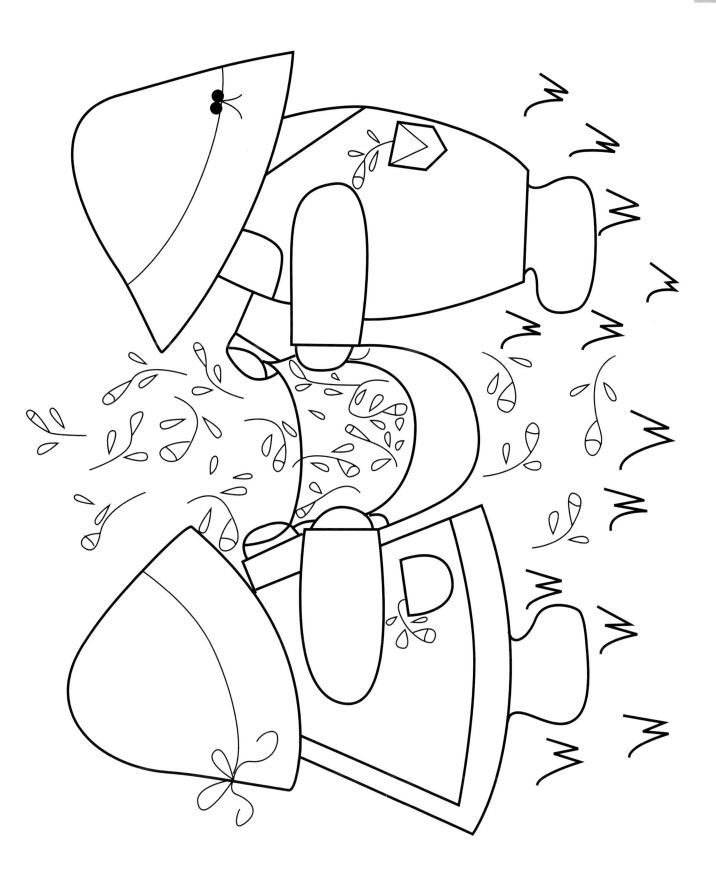

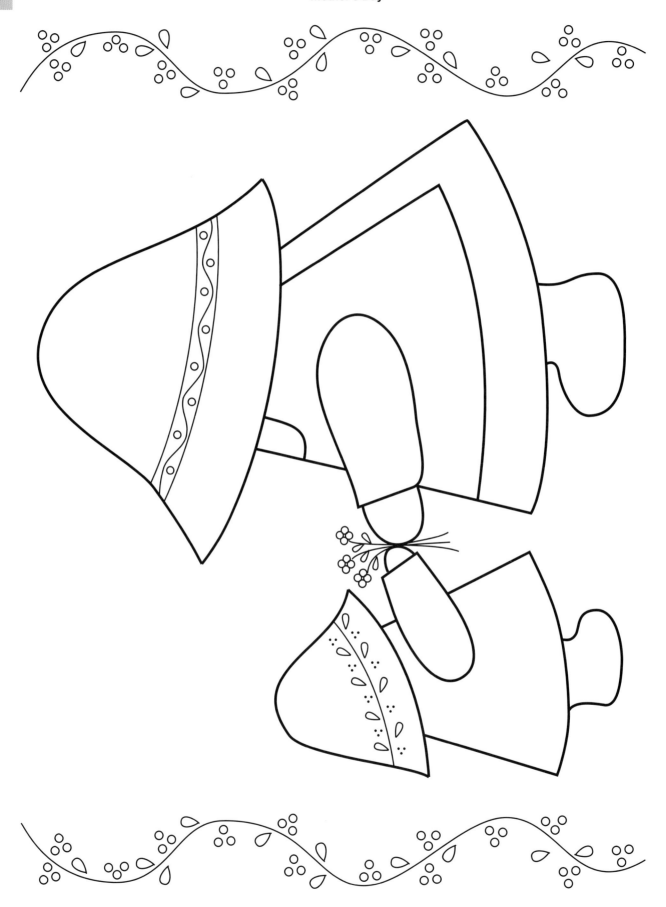

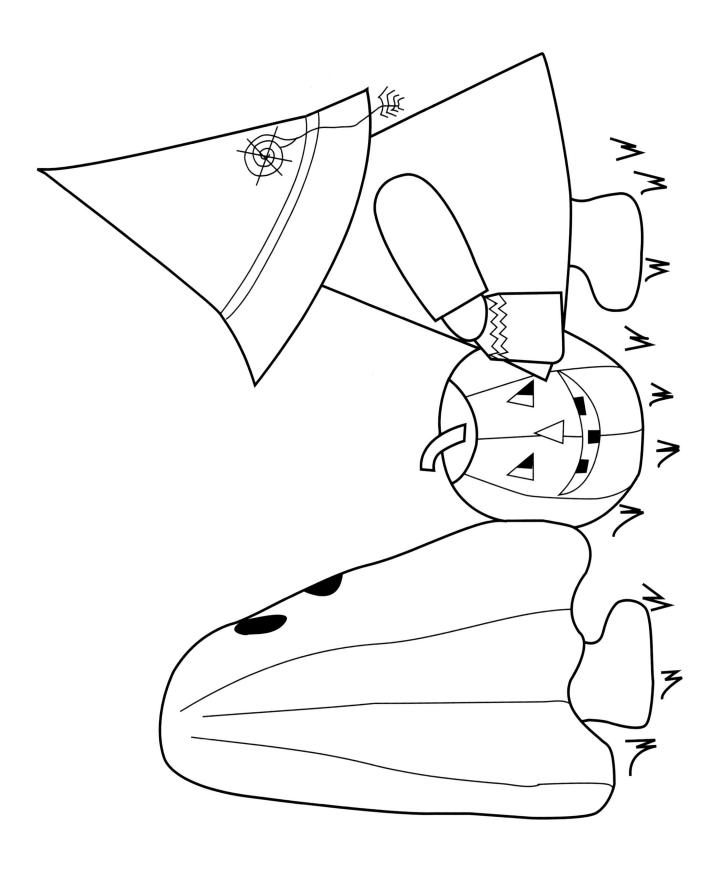

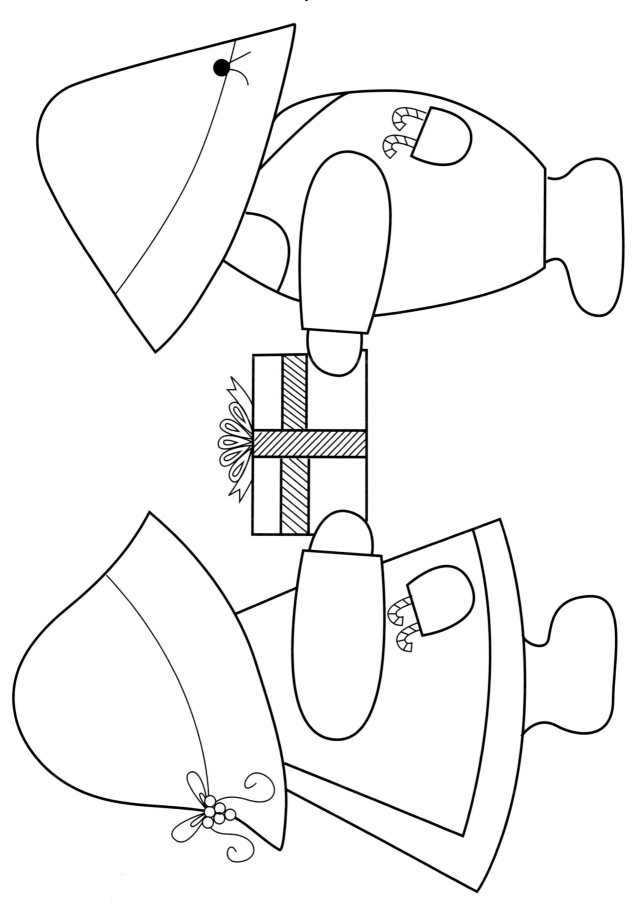

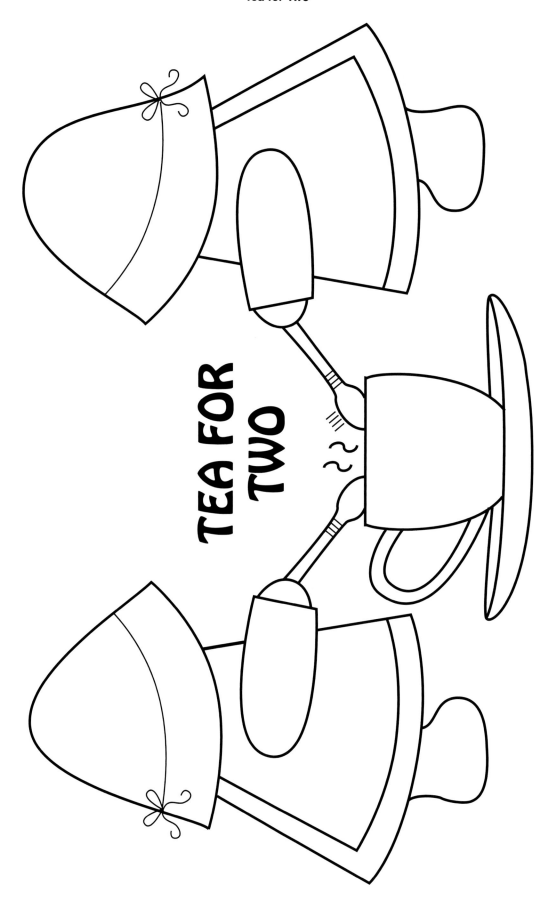

HOUSE OF WHITE BIRCHES, BERNE, INDIANA 46711 WWW.WHITEBIRCHES.COM

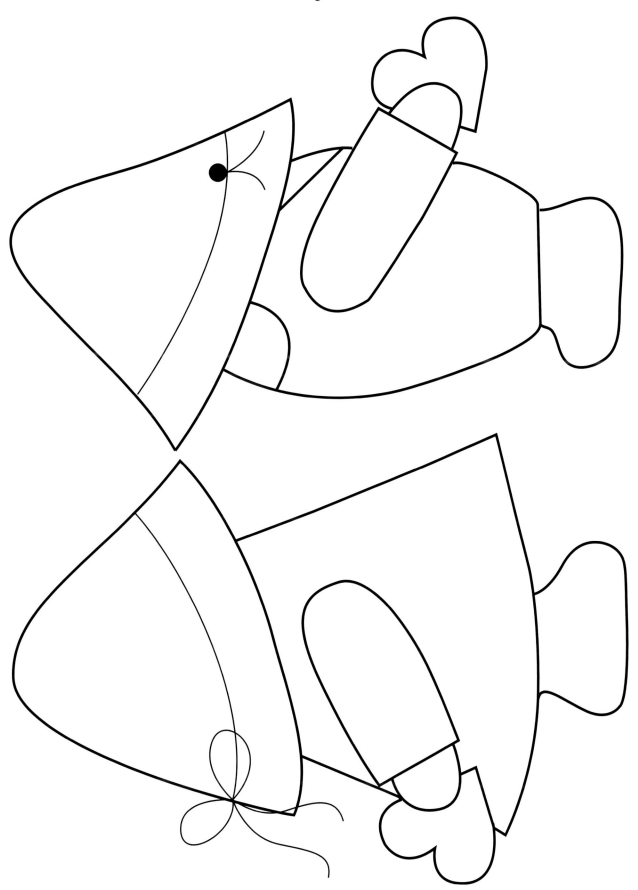

E-mail: Customer_Service@whitebirches.com

HOUSE of WHITE BIRCHES PUBLISHERS SINCE 1947

Fun With Sue & Sam is published by House of White Birches, 306 East Parr Road, Berne, IN 46711, telephone (260) 589-4000. Printed in USA. Copyright © 2005 House of White Birches.

RETAILERS: If you would like to carry this pattern book or any other House of White Birches publications, call the Wholesale Department at Annie's Attic to set up a direct account: (903) 636-4303. Also, request a complete listing of publications available from House of White Birches.

Every effort has been made to ensure that the instructions in this pattern book are complete and accurate. We cannot, however, take responsibility for human error, typographical mistakes or variations in individual work.

STAFF
Editors: Jeanne Stauffer, Sandra L. Hatch
Associate Editor: Dianne Schmidt
Technical Artist: Connie Rand
Copy Supervisor: Michelle Beck,
Copy Editors: Nicki Lehman,
  Beverly Richardson
Graphic Arts Supervisor: Ronda Bechinski

Graphic Artists: Debby Keel, Edith Teegarden
Art Director: Brad Snow
Assistant Art Director: Nick Pierce
Photography: Tammy Christian, Carl Clark,
  Christena Green, Matthew Owen
Photo Stylists: Tammy Nussbaum,
  Tammy Smith

Cover project: Appliqué by Neva Pharr; embroidery and quilting by Barb Dynes.

ISBN: 1-59217-054-4
1 2 3 4 5 6 7 8 9